Classroom Perspectives

STRATEGIES FOR STUDENT MANAGEMENT

By: Sharon R. Berry, Ph.D.

Created and Developed by
Christian Academic
Publications and Services, Inc.

Author	Sharon R. Berry, Ph.D.
Production	Sherry Berry
	Sandy Kilgo

LifeWay™

Published by
LifeWay Christian School Resources
127 Ninth Avenue North
Nashville, TN 37234-0182
1-800-458-2772
www.lifeway.com

ISBN: 0-6330-3528-9
Dewey Decimal Classification: 377
Subject Heading: DISCIPLINE, STUDENT MANAGEMENT,
CHRISTIAN SCHOOLS – CHURCH EDUCATION

CONTENTS

Contents

Building Schools of Influence
Committed to Kingdom Education

Whether one is a parent raising a child or a teacher in a school or church, everyone involved in teaching knows the importance of good classroom management. There have been many attempts to provide quick fixes to discipline problems faced by those who teach. However, a look at our society proves that quick fixes don't work. Children and youth need to experience Biblical discipleship from their teachers if they are going to become what Christ desires them to be.

Strategies for Student Management is the first book in a series of resources designed to give Christian teachers valuable perspectives concerning their call from God to influence young hearts and minds for eternity. In this book, one will discover God's unique plan for students to be nurtured to maturity so that they can become equipped unto every good work.

As you study the various topics, I warn you not to jump too quickly to many practical suggestions that are contained in these pages. Instead, prayerfully read the various essays, asking God to give you wisdom on how to develop classroom management strategies that will be effective. Any teacher can be confident that effective classroom management can be a reality if God's Word forms the foundation for all we do in training up a child.

I would also encourage you to study the second book in the ***Classroom Perspectives*** series entitled, ***Teachers Committed to Excellence***. May God richly bless you as you fulfill the high calling of being a teacher of future generations.

For the Kingdom,
Glen Schultz, Ed.D.
Manager, LifeWay Christian School Resources

For more information on these resources contact LifeWay Christian School Resources, 127 Ninth Avenue, N., Nashville, TN 37234 or call customer service at 1-800-458-2772.

Essay 1:

CHRISTIAN PERSPECTIVES ON CLASSROOM MANAGEMENT

"His divine power has given to us all things that pertain to life and godliness, through the knowledge of Him who called us by glory and virtue."
(2 Peter 1:3 NKJV)

If surveys are correct, classroom management continues to be the singular most important topic of interest among teachers. Whether inexperienced or a veteran of many years, if you are like other teachers, how to maintain a constructive learning environment while administering good discipline is the greatest challenge you face. Given the history and sheer enormity of the educational process in the United States, you would think that this topic would have been studied to its fullest and that a teacher would only need to glean from the experience of others in order to develop the expertise needed for daily success. Unfortunately, this isn't the case. With thousands of books available on the subject and innumerable "experts" dispensing advice, many teachers still struggle to develop effective keys to successful classroom management.

There are many reasons for this struggle. First is simply that teaching is a dynamic process that reflects differences in students and teachers from year to year, and even day to day. It is not a mechanical conveyor—rather, it is life interacting with life. Emotions, abilities, desires, motivations, moods, momentary ups and downs, all affect these interactions so that no two situations are ever exactly the same. Thus, good techniques of classroom management must grow from an underlying philosophy, not from "quick fixes" or "magical formulas" that address outward behaviors in a superficial manner.

A second reason is the continuous shift in cultural values. Techniques that worked when a society valued obedience to authorities and commitment to corporate good do not work in an environment where the rights of individuals and freedom of expression are highly valued by students' parents. Thus the process of classroom management often reflects the prevailing directions of society in general.

Actually, all systems of classroom management emanate from an underlying philosophy or belief system regarding the nature of children and the teaching-learning process. Historically, at least three distinct philosophies have influenced how teachers interacted with students. These are authoritarian, child-centered and behavioristic.

In an authoritarian framework the teacher was assumed to have all power and all knowledge. Students were to memorize and recite a prescribed amount of information. Discipline tended to be harsh in an effort to set an example for others. Daily routines were strictly followed and little attention was given to emotions or personal interactions. In fact, undue focus on self was seen as devil inspired. The role of education was to counter this influence as students were trained in acceptable moral behavior.

Early in the 20th century a more humanitarian (humanistic, some would say) approach to the education of children emerged. Promoted by John Dewey, Horace Mann and others, this child-centered philosophy saw children as having a spark of divinity—an internal sense of goodness—which only needed the opportunity to be revealed. Educational programs reflected this philosophy as they allowed students to pursue their own interests with little demand to demonstrate competence in skills or mastery of subject content. The role of the teacher was to guide, influence and encourage while providing an educational atmosphere for discovery and self-enhancement.

A competing philosophy developed during the years America transitioned from an agrarian society to an industrial revolution. Children were seen as products, the result of external conditioning and reinforcement of behaviors deemed admirable by society. Deriving from animal studies, a whole philosophy of behaviorism exerted enormous influence on the structure of classrooms in America. Through the efforts of B. F. Skinner and others, a child exhibiting a behavior problem needed only to have that behavior observed, measured and manipulated by consequences. Little consideration was given to internal motivation since it could not be observed and measured. In response to this philosophy, teachers became much more concerned with task analysis, mastery learning and contingency schedules.

It must be noted that philosophies seldom exist in schools in their purest forms. You are more likely to see amalgamations within individual teachers, as well as in the differences between various staff members. More current trends are a blend of approaches that seem, at heart, to be more child-centered in their emphasis on discipline with dignity, empowerment of students, etc. At the same time they recognize the right of teachers to benevolently direct and control the educational environment as they protect the rights of students to be safe and free to learn. While not as strict as some of the original behavior modification techniques, teachers continue to use a variety of positive and negative reinforcers, time out and behavior contracts.

Thus we are brought back to the critical issue of the difficulties a Christian teacher faces in finding a "tried and true" approach to classroom management. Beyond some restrictions imposed by a school or church's policies, teachers seem left to their own ingenuity in developing a system that works best in their classrooms.

Christian teachers face an even greater challenge, perhaps one they have not really consciously considered. That is their Biblical perspective on the nature of children and the nature of the teaching-learning process. Many Christian teachers have been trained in various forms of educational psychology, usually in secular university settings or by professors trained in these settings. They have not taken the time to deeply consider the teachings of Scripture and the differences a Biblical worldview might impose on their systems of discipline.

Knowing that behavior is born out of a belief system, teachers owe it to themselves to develop a truly Biblical approach to classroom management. In other words, what does Scripture say about the nature and treatment of children, about the responsibilities of those who train them, and about the process of discipline. This book provides an introduction to this topic that only "scratches the surface" as it presents a number of essays that address various Biblical topics. Interwoven with these essays are lots of suggestions related to specific application. These are generally organized from less specific to more specific intervention; they do not necessarily relate to the topic of an essay.

The book should serve you in at least two ways. The essays will provide a thoroughly Christian perspective on the subject of discipline or management of students in your classroom. The suggestions are meant to provide a ready resource of ideas. They will be useful as you consider your classroom, your methods of teachings, your interactions with students, your prevention of problems, your intervention when problems occur, and your need to seek outside support. As such, you may want to keep the book near your desk as an available guide when you need some fresh ideas. The suggestions have grown from more than 35 years of teaching experience filtered through the counsel of God's Word.

My desire for you is to be "thoroughly furnished unto good works, a workman who does not need to be ashamed." I am excited for you to embark on this approach to wisdom-based classroom management. May you be blessed as you seek His thoughts then successfully train students to be more like the Master.

Starting Right

Recognize that the essentials for good classroom management are routines and relationships. Both of these must be consistently maintained in order for students to become partners in the learning process.

The lack of routines leads to chaos which, in turn, leads to a basic sense of insecurity. Students then engage in repeated battles to define the limits. The more you can establish your classroom as a place of order, peace, purpose and direction, the better learners your students will become.

Start before the year begins. Consider the flow of traffic, sufficient storage, access of supplies and equipment, quiet areas versus busier areas, your vantage point, etc. Set up the classroom in ways that decrease confusion.

Think through regular routines of class—entering, leaving, obtaining permission, obtaining supplies, passing papers, options for free time, storing items, cleaning, lining up, walking in the

halls, playground times, etc.,—and be prepared to discuss your expectations during the
firstodays students report to class.
Incorporate any routines that are standard for
your department or grade level. While it's a
good idea to write these for yourself (and
later to give to substitute teachers), don't
overwhelm students with too many rules.
These are simply routines that have sufficient
similarity and regularity to facilitate a class of
students living together in harmony.

Decorate the room in a warm, person-
able style. However, don't go over-
board since it may distract students.
It's better to start with the essentials
and add items throughout the year. Be
acutely aware of the visual impression your
classroom makes. Don't let it be sloppy or
visually disconcerting. It should immediately send the message that your class exists for
the business of learning—inviting but calm
and purposeful.

Maintain a comfortable physical environment with good ventilation, control of heat and cooling, limited dis-
tractions, etc. Students must have
fresh air and water (six cups during the day)
for their brains to work efficiently. Be sure
both are available.

Plan some "getting to know you" activities to implement during the first days and weeks of class.

- name tags for everyone
- introductions focused on special talents or likes
- bulletin board or information sheets containing personal information
- a game where students must fill out grids with names—for example, someone whose family took a mission trip during the summer, takes piano lessons, likes broccoli, etc.
- buzz group where three or four students share information then introduce one another to the class
- an after-class outing for refreshments with small groups of students
- a "welcome back to class" party

Assign areas to students for personal belongings. They should not feel like a visitor to your classroom, but accept ownership as their classroom. Make adequate room for their storage and work space. This will produce both a sense of belonging and order.

Focus on Relationships

Speak to students as they enter the room. Refer to news of interest to them. Call their names often as you are teaching throughout the day.

Develop warm, caring relationships with all your students. Show your interest in their personal lives, especially their problems and questions. Be sure they perceive the love of God in you (John 13:35).

Make it a habit to have personal interaction time with each student. For elementary school students, plan for a brief time every day. For older students who change classes, make it your goal to speak personally with each student sometime during the week. For students you see periodically, such as Bible classes, Sunday School, clubs, etc., block some quality time for this purpose during each session.

Pray consistently for each student. Pray even more for those students who seem unteachable. It is possible that they hold the greatest potential for

future service. If you study the lives of effective preachers and missionaries, many of them
were very strong-willed children. It seems
God uses that type personality to pioneer new
works and take the risks necessary to attempt
new challenges for Him.

13 Learn what it takes to make each student feel accepted, significant and
appreciated rather than rejected or
even non-existent. Communicate to
your students God's interest, care and concern
for them as individuals.

14 Communicate an ideal for your class.
Share with them your vision for the
care and harmony that you anticipate
occurring in the class. Encourage students who act in accordance with this ideal.

15 Treat your students' parents as partners.
You have no better ally, no person more
interested in a student's well-being and
good performance, and no person more
dedicated to seeing that a student reaches his or
her potential.

16 Remember that you serve as a parent, a
"parentis en locus," meaning to be in the
place of a parent. Just as a mom and
dad must communicate in ways that
share concerns, not blaming or attacking one

another, you always want your messages to transmit great care, deep concern, willingness to work together to solve problems and long-term commitment.

17 To become successful, students must sense that they are capable, that they can connect to teachers and classmates, and that they can contribute to the group in a significant way. The more you convey the message of their significance, their belonging and their positive participation, the less they must struggle to achieve their needs in counterproductive ways.

18 Students are seeking five things in your class: acceptance, attention, appreciation, affirmation and affection. These are legitimate needs that are incorporated into the Biblical term "admonish." Fulfilling them communicates that students are loved and have purpose in the world. Practice your manner of speech and interactions to ensure that you convey these attitudes. Check for eye contact, gentle voice quality, respect, recognition of individuals, being inclusive not exclusive, etc.

How can you communicate that you really care for students? Try some of the following:

- follow up on prayer requests
- call names often
- compliment students to others
- check on any absent student
- speak to students outside of class, in the lunchroom or at the mall
- join into student activities such as games on a rainy day
- call parents to compliment a student's display of Christlike character
- recognize birthdays or other special events
- attend ball games or recitals
- have dinner with a student's family
- eat with students
- display special bulletin boards focusing on the student of the week—his family and activities
- send cards, notes or other messages just because you care
- ask about a special interest or a person important to the student
- make and share a treat such as brownies or bookmarks
- invite students for special outings or parties
- make time for individual students to conference or read to you

Essay 2:

"And, ye fathers, provoke not your children to wrath: but bring them up in the nurture and admonition of the Lord." (Ephesians 6:4 KJV)

Preachers call it a proof text—the foundational teaching on a particular subject in the Word of God. For parents and teachers, the verse is Ephesians 6:4. All that we know about rearing emotionally secure, competent children is summarized in this verse. Therefore, it's a good place to focus our study. Furthermore, after the foundations are laid, the principles of this verse will continue to unfold as our study progresses.

The verse can be considered in four parts. First there is a negative command translated in a variety of ways both here and in its companion verse, Colossians 3:21:

- *Do not exasperate your children.*
- *Do not provoke your children to anger.*
- *Do not provoke your children lest they become discouraged or lose heart.*
- *Do not embitter your children.*

A negative command in Scripture always indicates a high likelihood that we naturally disobey God's standard in this area. Thus it is important for us to take a long look at the ways we frustrate and anger our students if we are going to be obedient to His Word. This will occur throughout the book as we study good classroom management principles.

The positive command of Ephesians 6:4 simply says we are to bring children up. The word in the original language means to grow or nurture. It is a horticulture term much like you would use to describe the growing of plants and flowers. With gardening as a hobby and 38 years experience nurturing children, I am convinced that the two activities have a lot in common. Both need nutrition, good soil, sunshine and rain. Both need deep roots and room to grow. Both have their natural growth cycles. Both need protection against weeds and invading insects that can easily destroy a young, tender stem. Both need the removal of "suckers" that sap strength and fruitfulness. Occasionally, both need to be staked and bound to grow tall and straight. Gardening requires patience during the time needed for a small seed to transition from a tender plant to a fruitful vine. Teaching also requires patience knowing that growing children is a day-by-day adventure.

The last part of Ephesians 6:4 tells us the two foundational elements related to growing children into happy, productive adults. At first glance the words used in the King James Version appear opposite to our expectations. The word "admonition" seems to be the harsher term meaning "warning, penalty, scolding, punishment, etc." However, the same word is used in Colossians 3:16, "Let the word of Christ dwell in you richly in all wisdom, teaching and admonishing one another in psalms and hymns and spiritual songs, singing with grace in your hearts to the Lord."

In reality, the word means encouraging, uplifting, total acceptance. It refers to that positive side of teaching where we develop relationships that genuinely show our appreciation for the children that God has loaned to us. Thus, the first foundational stone of good teaching is love. In our classrooms, love translates to acceptance, respect, attention, communication of worth, purpose and potential, making students feel that they belong, sharing success and overcoming failure. It means all the positive interactions you have that reflect the love of God into their lives.

The second term, "nurture," is variously translated discipline, training, direction, structure or control. It is the stricter of the two terms and conveys the second foundational stone of good classroom management. Students must have environments characterized by a constancy and consistency that produce a bedrock of emotional security. Students who are emotionally secure thrive under teachers who establish the rules, are predictable and fair in applying them, are trustworthy, keep their promises and meet their students' needs, emotional as well as physical and mental. The presence of emotional security protects students from neurotic fears and anxieties. It enables students to reach out and take risks as they fulfill the God-given potential for their lives.

This is ground zero—two foundational stones from which all other issues of classroom management emerge.

If we are to grow emotionally healthy, competent students, we must build into them these two foundational characteristics. Thankfully, we are not left to our own devices in determining how to do the job right. We need only to rely on the nature and promises of our Lord. For example, 2 Timothy 1:7 says, "For God has not given us a spirit of fear, but of power, and of love and of a sound mind."

God is not the author of chaos, but of order. It is on the basis of His sovereignty that we can have complete security. Therefore, He has not given us the spirit of fear, anxiety or intimidation. Rather, He imparts power—not the TNT kind—but boulder-like strength that provides a sense of confidence and peace.

Second, we understand from Scripture that we are accepted in the beloved, without conditions or demands. We are just loved—fully and completely. On the basis of these two reflective characteristics of God, we are capable of right thinking (a sound mind) about who God is, who we are, how we belong to a family, as well as society at large, and what purposes God has for our service to Him and mankind.

Note some of the distinctive features of this verse. First is the dual and equal foundational building blocks of security and love. These are complementary, interactive sides of a single concept which ultimately reflects the nature of God. Based on experiencing the harmonious structure of security and love, a student can understand his value and relationship to his family, to himself (self-esteem) and to God. And he can conceptualize the potential value and place he has in the larger social structure of the world. With a sound mind—right thinking—he can strive to fulfill the wonderful plans and potential God has for his life.

Does this not make perfect sense? Once again we are challenged with the profound implications of Scripture. Already, God has given us all that is needed for life and godliness (2 Peter 1:3). Nowhere is this more true than in gaining the wisdom needed in teaching and training children. In conforming believers to the image of Jesus Christ, the Holy Spirit reproduces the nature of God in us. Does His nature not reflect absolute trustworthiness and unconditional love? Perhaps Psalm 63:11–12 (NIV) summarizes it best:

One thing God has spoken,
two things have I heard:
that you, O God, are strong,
and that you, O Lord, are loving.
Surely you will reward each person
according to what he has done.

God is strong, consistent and trustworthy. His nature is loving. Because He works to conform you to His image, these characteristics will become true of you as you mature in your relationship with Him. Thus, the expressions of these characteristics become a natural outgrowth of the fruit of the Spirit. More than learning a "few tricks of the trade," it is my prayer that you will grow to be more like the Master. In so doing, Biblically-based classroom management will become automatic as you respond to students in accordance with His nature.

Focus on Routines

Maintain an orderly, well-run class. This sets the stage for students to "go with the flow," as they automatically react to your expectations.

Insist on observing regular routines for every part of class—entering, sitting, answering questions, putting away books, getting pencils, etc. This doesn't have to be dictatorial, just calmly and consistently implemented. The process establishes a sense of well-being for students in that they know what to expect and know that the rights of all class members are protected. It will save you time in the long run and prevent arguments among students.

Use seating arrangements as a specific tool to achieve good management. It is not necessary to assign seats in every situation, but you will want to control the arrangement of chairs. Keep some seats empty for changing students as needed. During the first weeks, you may want to change seating arrangements occasionally until you find the one that works best for your class.

Define and post your non-negotiable rules for your class. Be definite but keep them few in number. Older students can help in listing them. Go through them occasionally as a normal part of class instruction. This allows you to remind students, refine any specific points and discuss problems. Refer to them as a part of class routine. For example, "Thanks for raising your hand, Sean. That's a rule we always observe in this class."

Praise students who follow the rules. Be specific. For example, "Good paying attention, Jamal." "Not talking when you pass out pencils is a real help to me, Bethany." Other reinforcers are smiles, pats, handshakes, thumbs up, smiling faces on a paper, stickers, stars, a personal note, an extra privilege, etc.

NOTES:

Model Order

Teach and live the principles of authority structure. Honor those in authority over you and carefully guard how students perceive your relationships with them. Be committed to your responsibility to live in accordance with God's Word and in harmony with other workers. Realize that learning to live under authority allows students to transition to the authority of God in their lives—but first, they must see it in your life.

Develop and exemplify personal self-discipline. Most good discipline is "caught" and not "taught" as students observe how you maintain your classroom, manage the instructional program, handle stress, develop positive relationships with others, keep a steady, even temperament and react well to problems and disappointments. Your students will never rise to higher levels of personal management than they see you demonstrate in your class.

Be organized. Have a place for everything. Stick to a schedule. Have all materials handy. Proceed smoothly

NOTES:

from one activity to another. Keep things clean and neat as you go. Put things back into their assigned places after using them.

28. Get rid of clutter. It's better to have two pencils sharpened and ready than 14 you must sort through every time one is needed. The same is true for other supplies and teaching materials. Dispense with broken items. Give away items you have not used within the last year.

29. Prepare for class in advance so that students will have enough work to do for the various periods of instruction. Always have handy some alternate plans and materials. Remember the advice: Plan your work and work your plan. At the same time, be flexible enough so that if you are unable to accomplish all you had hoped, you do not become frustrated. Sometimes, the Spirit will lead you to attend to a need that arises on the spur of the moment. That's okay as long as the general flow of the class is predictable.

30. Be early for class, have all materials ready, and greet every student by name at the door. Direct students to immediate action by assigning them to an area, a task or to begin the morning routine.

Demonstrate leadership. Be definite. Be in control. Be directive. You are the teacher and the students look to you for guidance. They are quick to pick up indecisiveness, disorganization, etc. If you do not control the flow of the class, students automatically will. Lack of good preparation and clear directions are open invitations for problem behaviors to erupt.

NOTES:

Essay 3: THE DEMAND FOR ORDER

"Let all things be done decently and in order."
(I Corinthians 14:40 NKJV)

The need for a consistent, safe environment (both physically and emotionally) continues throughout the school years. Your responsibility in nurturing children is to establish a climate in which students feel secure. This is not the result of things serendipitously falling into place, but of careful planning and implementation. A wise educator once said, "Teaching is a constant stream of decision-making. Teach by design, not by accident." Your trustworthiness is communicated by your being in control, well planned, organized, directive, respectful of others' rights and under authority.

In like manner, your classroom must be a place of calmness, order, routine and consistent application of the rules. Without this secure environment your students will constantly challenge the limits as they struggle with their own sense of anxiety. If you are to be an effective teacher, developing your classroom as a place to feel secure and accepted is not optional—it is mandatory.

Can you do it? Is it possible to achieve an ordered, consistent, peaceable classroom? Absolutely! But not because of us—because of

Him. God's nature provides for us the model of strength and security. Think about the descriptors repeated throughout Scripture.

- He is my rock, the God of my salvation.
- He is my fortress, the strength of my life.
- He is the anchor of the soul.
- He is the solid foundation.
- Sovereign, immutable,
- The same yesterday, today and forever.
- He says, "I change not."

God alone is absolutely and ultimately trustworthy. Without doubt or fear, we know that He is in control. His actions are firm, directed and according to plan. He created a world that reflects His nature, that operates in accordance with mathematical and scientific principles so precise and predictable that men can circle the moon and return to an exact destination. The sun rises and sets, the tides ebb and flow, all according to His time schedule. On a more personal level, He consistently meets our needs and satisfies the deepest longings of our hearts.

God's plan, actually His passion, is for Christians to be conformed to His image. He desires to make us trustworthy, peaceable, orderly, consistent human beings that reflect His nature. So, is it possible to achieve this lifestyle? Absolutely! But not because of us—because of Him. Let's take heart from His Word.

"Behold, God is my salvation; I will trust, and not be afraid, for the Lord, is my strength and my song; he also is become my salvation." (Isaiah 12:2)

"His divine power has given us everything we need for life and godliness through our knowledge of him who called us by his own glory and goodness. Through these he has given us his very great and precious promises, so that through them you may participate in the divine nature." (2 Peter 1:3–4 NIV)

Isaiah wrote, "And the work of righteousness shall be peace; and the effect of righteousness, quietness and assurance forever. And my people shall dwell in a peaceable habitation, and in sure dwellings, and in quiet resting places" (32:17–18). This is your promise as you make the effort to ensure that your classroom is a safe, peaceable, sure dwelling place. In turn, your students will develop a sense of emotional security that provides a strong foundation upon which to build a productive life.

Engender Respect

Insist on respect for adults. Students should address you by title and last name. In some situations, a title and first name is acceptable. Honor visitors to your class. Make time to practice proper interactions between students and other adults.

Also insist that students show respect for one another. Implement a basic principle for your class—what is right for one is right for all. Here are a couple of examples.

1) The rule is: Obtain permission before talking. Why? Because if one student insists on talking, it must be inherently right for every class member to talk. If everyone talks, chaos will result and no learning will be accomplished. For the benefit of, and fairness to, every member, we observe the rule.

2) A student treats a peer unkindly. In discussing your concerns you emphasize that you would not allow others to treat him in a similar way. In fact, you will make sure

NOTES:

that others show respect and that he will be protected. Therefore, you will not allow him to treat others in ways that are hurtful, either physically or emotionally.

Set the tone of your class by being respectful in your interactions with students. Avoid at all costs a critical edge to your voice, a critical spirit, talking down, laughter at someone's expense, correction in front of others, assuming an evil intent on the students' part, or punishing the group for the misbehavior of a few. A teacher is responsible to build up, not tear down.

*Develop an Engaging
Teaching Style*

35 Know your material, its organization for most efficient teaching, and the methods that best convey it. This is difficult for a beginning teacher, but your goal is to so thoroughly know the content of each subject that it becomes second nature. Your primary focus is then on getting students engaged with the material and on monitoring the learning process.

36 Present interesting, age-appropriate lessons. No matter how well you have planned your information, materials and methods, if they are not appropriate to the maturity and interests of your class, you invite problem behaviors.

37 Follow good lesson planning format.

1) Engage interest, create a need to know, present a problem that needs a solution, provide time for students to fail and thus be motivated to learn. This is the time for discovery learning.

2) Build a bridge to previously learned material. This process awakens previously

activated channels of neurons in the brain
and prepares them to add to the memory
patterns already established.

3) Present new material. This is the time
for directed teaching. You want to present
information in an organized manner that
builds on previously learned material.
Whatever methodologies are used, the goal
is the same—to connect the dots between
what I know and what I need to know.

4) Students engage in supervised practice
or in personal consideration of the meaning
and importance of what was learned.

5) Students engage in unsupervised practice
or in personal application of the material.

6) Students rehearse what was learned and
why it is important.

Teach with style. Make your presentations lively and student-involved with
variety in methods, visuals and materials. Don't fall into the habit of doing
the same thing again and again. While the
organization of your classroom should be
routine, being able to predict the flow of a
lesson (read paragraph 27, discuss it; read
paragraph 28, discuss it) delivers a death
blow to motivation for learning.

Be careful about over-stimulation. Too much variety in one lesson is not good because it does not allow you to focus on a single theme and application. Do not use material that requires a lot of time or causes confusion in its manipulation. Too many physical activities can result in bedlam very quickly, particularly if there is not a natural connection to the material being taught.

Engage students in the learning process. In research related to retention after 24 hours, the selected methodologies produced the following percentages of material remembered.

Teacher lecturing alone	5%
Students reading while teacher lectures	10%
Audio-visual presentation with lecture	20%
Demonstration with lecture	30%
Discussion group after presentation	50%
Personal practice	75%
Teaching others or other immediate use	90%

Watch your timing. According to research, the ideal lessons occur in about a 20-minute time period. During this time, the first few minutes are prime for learning. At about 10 to 12 minutes, interest will begin to wane. At 20 to 22 minutes, it is best to use the next 8 to 10 minutes of down-time for rehearsal or practice. You can then switch topics or pick up the next segment of your lesson and repeat the process.

Eliminate the boredom that can result from tedious repetition and busy work. Learning traces in the brain are enhanced by repetition with novelty. This simply means that some new aspect should be present each time information is repeated. Remember that most paper-pencil tasks can be easily reworked to manipulatives, flash cards and game formats.

Assemble an idea file for time-fillers, "minute maximizers," when you are cleaning up, changing activities, waiting in line, etc. For example, match states and capitals, repeat math facts, name the muscles of the body, say the books of the Old or New Testament, say Bible verses, name favorite songs, or play guessing games like, "I'm thinking of what God made, it is in the sky, it is soft and fluffy" or "I'm thinking of the area of the brain that processes emotional messages."

Ask questions that require students to use higher order thinking skills such as comparisons, contrasts, analysis, application and evaluation. After each question, institute "think time." In other words, you want a quality answer, not just a quick one. After several seconds, ask those who want to contribute to raise their hands.

All students have different learning styles and unique strengths and weaknesses. As you provide variety in your instructional program, be sure you are incorporating materials which balance between those who learn sequentially and those who learn globally, those who learn visually and those who learn auditorily. Teacher styles of learning usually represent the minority of students in a class. Therefore, you must make effort to broaden your methodology to reflect the various intelligences and styles your students naturally engage in order to learn.

Students are often caught between our expectations for them to be quiet and submissive and our desire for them to show initiative, creativity, independence, leadership, elaboration, etc. These traits can only be engendered in environments that allow voice and choice. We are created with an internal drive to fulfill the first commandment from God—to establish dominion over our life arenas. To help students achieve this goal, maximize times they can participate in sharing ideas, making decisions, working while self directed, and bearing ownership of the final outcomes.

NOTES:

Essay 4: THE DESIRE FOR LOVE

"To the praise of the glory of His grace, by which He has made us accepted in the Beloved."

(Ephesians 1:6 NKJV)

A theologian was once asked, "What is the greatest truth of all Scripture?" After a moment of thoughtful hesitation, he replied, "That Jesus loves me." And so it is that "God demonstrates His own love toward us, in that while we were still sinners, Christ died for us" (Romans 5:8). We did not earn or deserve His love; we have done no good thing. But God, through the sacrifice of Himself in His Son, extended His great love for our good. On this basis we can return to John's question: If God so loved us, should we not show this same love to others? In the same way that our Heavenly Father provides for His children's well-being, we are responsible to provide for the "benefit, profit, wealth, good or well-being" of the students assigned to us. Children need to perceive themselves as objects of unfailing love which is never conditional on anything they do or don't do. It is simply "I accept you as God's gift. I love you because you are you."

We need to start with a common definition of our subject. For our purposes, love is an unreserved, undeserved acknowledgment, acceptance and appreciation for a student's presence. It leads a teacher to expend himself to provide for the benefit of his students. Some terms that aid our understanding of this kind of love include:

accept	develop a relationship with	develop a belongingness
appreciate	care for	edify
esteem	be loyal to	admonish
bond to	encourage	build up
value	assign significance to	seek good for
attribute worth to	nurture	share time with
give attention	cherish	give priority to
act in benefit of	communicate with	
sacrifice for	display interest in	

Because we claim the name and nature of Christ, we are challenged to let His mind be in us. This is especially true in understanding the esteem Jesus had for children and His teachings about how they should be treated. Matthew 18:1–6 and 10–14 serve as the premier verses on the subject. In answer to the disciples' question regarding who would be greatest in the kingdom of God, Jesus clearly demonstrates His attitude toward children.

(Who is greatest . . . ?) ⟶ (He called a little child.)

His following commands are fairly simple to understand, but more of a challenge to consistently practice. Consider the following ones:

"Welcome in My name." In Scripture, name is related to nature. Therefore, Jesus clearly commanded that we emulate His nature in our treatment of children—esteeming them worthy, gently embracing them, accepting them as they are, appreciating their inherent natures, having a vision and passion for their future. Note that in similar fashion to Jesus' later statement, "whatever you do for the least of these my brothers, you have done to me," He implies that whoever welcomes children, welcomes Him. As a Christian teacher you have no higher calling than involvement in a ministry that is so near to the heart of God.

"Do not offend." Similar to Ephesians 6:4, we encounter a negative command, one so serious that Jesus said it would be far better to be drowned in the deepest sea than to offend even one little child. To mistreat a child is to mistreat Jesus Himself. Have you done anything recently that did not reflect the nature of Jesus? Have you offended the heart of a child, causing him to think, "If a Christian is like that, I don't want any part of it"? These are serious questions that deserve contemplative responses.

"Don't look down on or despise." The opposite of love is not hate, it's rejection. Jesus forbids us from considering these little ones as though they had no worth, to disregard their needs or overlook their value. Children are so important to God that His angels are given watch over them. Sometimes our error in relating to students is not so much maltreatment as it is to neglect their care, or fail to mold them to the high purposes of God.

"Don't lose even one." Some of the greatest evangelistic sermons of all time feature a shepherd who leaves 99 safe in the fold to seek for one lost, wandering lamb. This scene is the subject of many hymns and great works of art. It doesn't lessen its broader application to realize that this story is told in the context of Jesus' discourse of the value of children. The conclusion to the parable is, *"It is not the will of your Father who is in heaven that one of these little ones should perish."*

Jesus' life and teachings exemplify the attitude we must have toward children. It is through our communication of their intrinsic value as created in the image of God and beloved by their Father that they sense a positive personal identity. Thus, love forms the second foundational block of growing into emotionally healthy, competent adults. The two bedrock boulders—emotional security and love—are represented in the nature of God Himself. As Christian teachers and parents, we are responsible to reflect that nature to the students entrusted to us.

Let there be no misunderstanding. This does not imply a catering to every whim and fancy a child may possess, coddling and pampering a spoiled brat. Instead, it is the calculated administration of a rational program that accomplishes benefit for the child. Some professionals have termed it "tough love" because it demands a teacher or parent to sometimes make what seems to be a very harsh decision, but that decision produces a desired positive outcome. Children who are accepted, taught and disciplined in love have ingrained into the internal fiber of their being a sense of right perspective toward themselves and their ability to make positive contributions to their world.

Motivate Learning

Students learn best when they assume ownership (responsibility) of what they learn. As often as possible, and when appropriate, incorporate them into decision making related to the educational process in your classroom. While you are responsible to direct the class in all matters that benefit and protect the corporate whole, many activities can be done as well one way as another. When this occurs, let students make choices individually, or exercise the democratic process by voting a choice for the class.

Regarding personal choices, provide lots of opportunities for students to select from among various assignments and activities. They will do best with what interests them and blends with their talents and styles of learning.

Rethink what students can do in lieu of, or in addition to, listen, read, write and memorize. Some actions to consider are:

act out	keep	**NOTES:**
analyze	list	
apply	look for	
ask	make	
assist	model	
build	name	
care about	order	
categorize	organize	
choose	outline	
classify	phone	
collect	plan	
compare	pray	
construct	realize	
control	record	
correspond	rejoice	
create	report	
demonstrate	research	
design	respond	
develop	restructure	
devise	role-play	
devote time to	save	
diagram	schedule	
direct	select	
discuss	sequence	
draw	share	
eliminate	show	
encourage others	sketch	
enjoy	stop	
evaluate	study	
exemplify	suggest	
exhibit	take	
experiment	talk to	
find	teach	
follow	tell	
give	think about	
go	use	
help	value	
identify	watch	
interview	witness	
invent	work on	

Focus on higher order thinking skills as you challenge students to stretch beyond simple memorization and identification of information. They are more motivated to learn material that has personal relevance. Help them make connections to real life.

Give your students something to work for. Well-motivated classes are far less likely to present discipline problems. A production for parents or a local nursing home, a field trip, a film can be appropriately related to your curriculum. Sometimes, non-educational rewards—a special treat, sleep over, even ten minutes of free time—are real motivators for students. Using a few motivation charts is fine, but be careful if they demonstrate the poor performance of two or three students; that will only cause more problems.

Provide opportunities for students to work in groups. Peer pressure can be a positive (and, yes, unfortunately, a negative) force for good behavior. Some teachers feel that taking time for group work reduces the amount of time they have to dispense information. Research supports the concept of being "fellow laborers" as beneficial to both the social and academic growth of students. Therefore, not taking time for group work may mean sacrificing depth of learning for breadth of exposure.

Watch for opportunities for even your most difficult students to accept responsible roles of leadership. This can often positively affect a student's attitude and behavior.

Provide lots of feedback to students so that they will know when they are meeting your expectations and when they are not. Explain specifically what it is that you are looking for and how your students are meeting your objectives. Do this especially when things are going well since it is easy to take these times for granted. When things are going less well, feedback is crucial: students cannot judge the behaviors that please you without your articulating clearly and kindly what they must do to improve.

Occasionally write notes on the board that provide feedback to students as to how things are going. Some possibilities are as follows:

- The kind of work you did today makes me glad to be a teacher.
- We had a really great day today.
- I can't imagine having a better class in the whole world.
- Keep up the good work and we will have a surprise on Friday.
- I feel so encouraged when you do

such a fine job.
- I especially appreciate the work you did in ____.

Once every several classes, as a closing activity of the day, ask students to help you evaluate how things are going. Some possible items to discuss are:

- some things we did that were tough
- some things we did that were really fun
- some things we did that we could have done better
- some things we would like to change
- some things we would like to repeat
- things I like about my class
- ways we can improve in the future.

*Keeping it
Positive*

Communicate the idea to your students that you are proud of what they are becoming. This keeps the focus on progress, not perfection. Get into the habit of providing encouragement such as: "I see you becoming more and more helpful to others." "It's good to see you progressing in your ability to obey quickly." "Your patience is improving. I can see differences from the time we started." "Keep this up and you will reach your goal of remembering to bring your assignments each time."

Have discussions on the kind of class students want to have. Do not allow students to call names such as, "If Brad would be quiet, our class would be fine." Instead, they should use general terms, such as, "No one should talk without permission." When this information comes from the students themselves, it provides strong peer pressure against a few who can be disruptive.

Devote class time to training students in the character traits and behaviors you expect. For example:

1) General politeness such as opening doors, letting others go first, waiting for people to exit an elevator before entering it, the difference in the inside voice and outside voice, being extra careful around elderly adults or younger children, etc.

2) Interacting with adults, making introductions, maintaining eye contact, answering questions, etc.

3) Pride in their learning environment such as picking up trash, cleaning up what is messed up, keeping things neat and in their place, taking care of equipment and facilities, etc.

 Devote class time to discussions regarding emotions. It is important that students identify their feelings and learn to manage them in positive ways. Explain that emotions are a wonderful gift from God. However, we are responsible for our response. That's why Ephesians 4:15 says, "Be angry and sin not." As their teacher, help them recognize their emotions and provide support while not changing your expectation for appropriate behavior.

Rally your students to service. Like the Dead Sea, any student who continually takes in "living water" but never gives

NOTES:

it out will develop a bitter, cantankerous spirit. Use projects to motivate and involve those
difficult students. They are often the ones
who show the greatest enthusiasm and leadership for such ministry opportunities.

Promote the study of biographies of
great people of character and achieve-
ment. Emphasize their commitment
to self-control and living by high
moral principles.

Lead students to deduce life principles
from your academic content.
Completing a simple page of math
problems provides potential discussion
of the following principles:

1) Having a plan or strategy increases effi-
ciency.

2) Repetition of a skill leads to better performance, whether learning math facts or
shooting basketballs.

3) Getting a perfect score is not always possible; doing my best is.

4) It is important to know how to correct
mistakes.

5) When you are conscientious in the smaller
things, the big things take care of themselves.

Don't do an overkill on every subject, but take several opportunities daily to help them see a "bigger picture" in how this information is important for relationships at home, with friends, with other subjects, etc.

 Always display courtesy to students as you maintain a pleasant voice and kind words. Remember that what you say is often less important than how it is said. Be careful of facial expressions and body language.

Be positive in your approach to students. Expect the best. Give encouragement and inspiration.

For no reason at all, write personal notes of appreciation and encouragement to various students and place them in students' desks, books or book bags. Have a system so that over time everyone receives a note.

Occasionally send positive notes sealed in envelopes to parents, and grandparents. Your students, even the high schoolers, will enjoy taking such notes home.

Build a history with your class with snapshots, samples of work, clippings of students' achievements, a class newsletter, etc. As a sense of "belonging" develops, students will bond to you and to each other.

Establish some star student days. This could be once a week or whatever works best for you. Encourage other students to write notes to the student or place a comment on a large card the class has designed. Add your own comments and close with a verse of Scripture which you feel characterizes this student. Place his collectibles in a memory bag to take home and share with parents.

Use true-life stories to illustrate behaviors you are trying to encourage. Although my husband and I answered questions and provided rationales when possible, our daughters were taught to obey immediately on command. One day we were water skiing when I quietly, but pointedly, told our younger daughter to get in the boat. She practically walked on water in response. Her instantaneous obedience may have saved her life as a poisonous snake surfaced about three feet from her. This story has often helped impress on students the importance of not questioning a command.

NOTES:

Involve students in decisions that affect them but are not critical to the flow of your classroom. For example, it's non-negotiable that they are to have writing time. However, it can be their decision as to whether it comes before or after morning snack. Let them help you with plans, projects, room decorations, preparations for special events, service projects, presentations, etc. Things will not always be perfect, but they will take pride in ownership as they gain confidence in their ability to contribute to the good of the whole class.

As you keep focused on positively affirming students, learn at least one hundred different ways to say, "That's good!" Some that work are:

Smart!	Exceeding
Doing good	expectations!
work!	Good thinking!
Awesome!	Good going!
Unbelievable!	Tremendous!
Championship	Fireworks!
material!	Perfect!
Daunting!	That's it!
Excellent!	Over the top!
Super!	Five-star effort!
Great!	Not bad!
Sensational!	Fantastic!
Spectacular!	Marvelous!
Superior!	Conscientious!
Prepared for	Good organiza-
success!	tion!

Evidence of good preparation!

That's better than ever!

Good response!

Blast off!

Accelerating rapidly!

Now you have it!

I knew you could do it!

How nice to see God working in you!

God's purpose for you!

The next time will be easier!

You're fulfilling your potential!

A workman, unashamed!

It's happening!

Coming along nicely!

Your performance is much better today!

You have outdone yourself!

You've got your brain in gear!

You make my job really fun!

You are on the right track!

You did some world-class work today.

Well, look at you!

What an improvement!

My! I'm pleased!

Intelligent!

Worthwhile!

Best performance yet!

Immeasurable progress!

Beyond measure!

Look at you go!

Shining bright!

Positively proud!

Wonderful!

Greatly appreciated!

Beautiful!

How did you get to be so smart?

Salt and light!

God is sure working through you!

Sehr gut (German)

Muy bueno (Spanish)

Tres bien (French)

Odlic no (Croatian)

A work of art!

A masterpiece!

Creative!

Your brain is working over-time!

Exhilarating!

Fascinating!

Surprised yourself, didn't you?

Deep thinking evidenced!
Very mature responses!
Award performance!
Worth talking about!
Your parents will be so proud!
Absolutely thrilling!
Shows lots of insight!
Achieving new heights!
Demonstrates good wisdom!
More consistent every day!
Hard job, well done!!
Unique performance!
Great person, great performance!
You went the extra mile!
Committed to excellence!
On the button!
Good choices!
A star is born!

Time to shout!
A caterpillar turned butterfly!
Especially nice!
Neato!
What a winner!
You've taken the prize!
Olympic performance!
First rate!
Delicious and delightful!
Doing it right!
Remarkable!
Extraordinary!
Giving it your best!
Leading the way!
Work of a prince (princess)!
On the road to success!
Stellar job!
Exquisite!
It's a pleasure to teach when you do so well!
Flying high!
Momentous!
More than a conqueror!
Just what I wanted!

NOTES:

Remember the truth that good discipline is developed out of long-term, caring relationships. Because relationships are emotional (not mental) in nature, provide lots of "I feel" messages to your students. Complete the following sentence with some of the words below: I feel _____ when I see you . . . .

absolutely ecstatic	so proud
extremely pleased	excited
challenged myself	rewarded
warm in heart	thankful
so full of joy	special
grateful to the Lord	fortunate
beyond description	
genuinely valued	
encouraged as a teacher	

Emphasize the truth of Philippians 4:19, "I can do all things through Christ who strengthens me."

• Reframe their "I can't" statements into "I could do it if I had more time . . . if I had help with spelling . . . if I had read the question correctly." Help them pinpoint specific areas for improvement that will eventually lead to success.

• Require at least one "I can" statement for an "I can't." For example, a student comes to your desk with the typical "I can't . . . ." Ask: "What is it that you can do?" Help the students build a bridge from their last success to the new challenge.

• With older students let them put their "I can't" statements on paper then nail them to a wooden cross, as if giving them to the Lord.

Recognize students for a character trait rather than appearance or performance. For example, it's better to say, "What a great choice of clothes you made today" rather than "You are so cute." Some traits to consider are:

attentiveness	dependability
attitude	determination
calmness	diligence
carefulness	discernment
caring	effort
cheerful spirit	encouragement
commitment	energy
concentration	enthusiasm
confidence	faithfulness
consideration	forgiveness
contentment	friendliness
cooperation	gentleness
courage	gracefulness
courtesy	graciousness
creativity	hard-working

heart for missions
heart for service
heart for the Lord
honesty
humility
humor
initiative
insight
integrity
joyfulness
kindness
leadership
loyalty
love
maturity
mercy
modesty
non-critical
obedience
optimism
organization
patience
peacefulness
perseverance
persistence

politeness
positive outlook
promise keeper
punctuality
reliability
reserve
respect
responsibility
reverence
self-control
sensitivity
serious concern
sincerity
strength of
   character
sympathy
tactfulness
thoroughness
thoughtfulness
tolerance
truthfulness
unselfishness
understanding
wisdom

NOTES:

Essay 5: BASIC BIBLICAL PRINCIPLES

"For whom the Lord loves He corrects, just as a father the son in whom he delights." (Proverbs 3:12 NKJV)

A helpful approach for Christian educators and parents to learn proper discipline techniques is to study how God disciplines His children. This can be done by checking the references for Bible terms like admonish, correct, chasten, reprove, rebuke, punish, upbraid, etc. Proverbs 3:11–12 states, "My son, do not despise the chastening of the Lord, nor detest His correction; for whom the Lord loves He corrects, just as a father the son in whom he delights." Thus God's dealings with the nation Israel, Old Testament saints, the New Testament Church, and with us today serve as an example of how we should deal with those we love and are responsible for. While not exhaustive, the following principles are demonstrated in God's program of discipline and are applicable to parents and teachers.

1) God clearly defines the rules and the consequences of obedience and disobedience. Adam and Eve knew exactly which trees were touchable and untouchable. They knew exactly the penalty for disobedience. Another clear example of this principle is in Deuteronomy 27 through 30 where Moses reviews the laws of God before the nation Israel which has camped in the shadows of Mount Gerizim and Mount Ebal. This

was God's object lesson that obedience brings blessing and rebellion brings curse. The nature of the written words of the Bible is to provide us a clear understanding of God's plan and our responsibilities. While we need not write an extensive dissertation for the operation of a classroom (God was content with ten commandments), we must provide clear expectations for our students' behaviors.

2) The strongest appeal for repentance and right living is the goodness of God. This is clear in Romans 2:4. In the same way, students are highly motivated by the examples set by their teachers in right living, patience, consistency and love. Most children really want to please the people who love them. When these significant adults are disappointed by a thoughtless, foolish act, a child deeply regrets their displeasure and is easily led to repentance and restitution. A positive, loving relationship is a great deterrent to discipline problems.

3) Chastisement is certain for disobedient children of God. Hebrews 12 provides an explanation of God's motivation—love. To allow a child to continue in disobedience is not in that child's best interests. God, therefore, extends Himself for our benefit to do whatever is necessary to ensure our return to the right way.

As a parent and teacher, I must honestly confess that many occasions arose in which I was tempted (yielding at times) to allow a misbehavior to simply "pass"—perhaps because it was easier to pick up a scrap of paper myself rather than giving the third reminder. Maybe I just dreaded another confrontation on what appeared to be slim evidence. Sometimes I was simply too worn out to do battle, and other times it just didn't seem worth the effort. The Lord had to really convict my heart in this area. While I never searched for problems or suspected wrongdoing, I promised the Lord that as He gave me knowledge of misbehaviors and negative attitudes, I would faithfully confront these issues with my children and students.

Others cannot afford to do less since our willingness to chasten when necessary is proof of our love. Only an uncaring teacher could ignore—or worse, encourage—development of behavior, attitudes and character traits that are in opposition to the plan of God.

4) God allows the occurrence of natural consequences for broken commandments. This is best illustrated in the process of sowing and reaping. While God lovingly forgives sins and restores fellowship, the scars often remain. Repentance does not necessarily achieve a cure for cirrhosis of the liver caused by alcohol abuse or a release from prison for a murder. The natural consequences of our sins remain, although God will sometimes graciously reduce their effects.

The temptation for teachers and parents is to intervene before natural consequences have the desired effect. This occurs in two ways. First, a teacher sometimes too hastily jumps into a situation with instruction or correction when the most effective teaching would have been natural conse-quences. This works particularly well with coats or lunch boxes left at home, equipment left on the playground, a mess left in the lunchroom, or inappropriate student interactions. Lessons for a lifetime are often learned when students must suffer for the choices they have made. Going without lunch, getting points off for lateness, having to clean up after others, on being embarrassed before peers are more effective than your lectures. Watch for occasions where these types of natural learning can occur.

The second way a teacher may wrongly intervene and short-cir-cuit the desired effects of natural consequences is after a child has shown remorseful repentance, especially if the teacher is feeling slightly guilty over some severe discipline. The teacher's natural reaction is "to make it all better." They will allow an extra day, substitute a project, agree to call parents or otherwise pitch in to help.

While all teachers will (and should) occasionally respond (in mercy) to help a student out of a jam, to consistently intervene teaches students to become overly dependent on authority figures and unable to function under ordinary frustrations (natural consequences) of life. Regardless of the circumstances or the costs, they believe that they can be excused from the system and feel unjustly treated when it doesn't happen. A student who does not learn to solve childhood problems will never learn to solve adult problems. Be careful to allow natural consequences to have their desired instructional effect for your students.

5) God patiently and repeatedly calls to repentance. The Old Testament is replete with God's call to repentance to the nation of Israel. The cycle of rebellion, sin, chastening, repentance and restoration occurs under Moses, the judges, the kings and the prophets. It would seem that either Israel might have learned a lesson or that God might have lost patience, but neither occurred. Rather, "The Lord . . . is longsuffering toward us, not willing that any should perish but that all should come to repentance" (2 Peter 3:9). The lesson for Christian teachers seems to be "Don't give up!" The days will get long. You may have to repeat the lesson the seventh (or the seven times seventieth) time; it may appear hopeless, but hang in there. Don't give up!

6) Repentance brings forgiveness and restoration without reminders of past sins. While many Bible characters (Abraham, David, the woman taken in adultery, John Mark, Paul) are illustrative of the principle, Jesus' treatment of Peter after his three denials serves as special encouragement to every Christian who has failed the Lord. While Peter's sin provided Jesus an opportunity to challenge him to service, there was no berating, stigmatism, ostracism or expectation of further failure.

James 1:5 says "If any of you lacks wisdom, let him ask God, who gives to all liberally and without reproach, and it will be given to him." This verse gives us two characteristics of God: He gives wisdom and He does not reproach. To reproach means to criticize severely, find fault with, upbraid, scold vehemently. This is a characteristic of Satan who is the accuser of the brethren. Even after our sins are forgiven, Satan delights in putting us under a heavy load of guilt and despair, wanting us to believe that we're no good, we will always fail, there is no use trying. God is never the one who lays this kind of heavy guilt on us. Rather, as Solomon said, "whoever confesses and forsakes them (his sins) shall have mercy." When a student has repented and made restitution, the whole matter must be forgotten.

A teacher may become aware of a pattern of misbehaviors occurring and may implement a program of prevention. Even then, the student should not be made to feel that "We're doing this because you have a problem." To continue holding a failure over a student's head only provides expectation for further failure. Even restrictions or accumulated punishments that are excessive and extend over a long period of time can create a negative image to which the student may conform. It is better to forgive and forget. While natural consequences may still be in effect, the sooner a student is restored to a right relationship with himself and others, the sooner he can continue the process of conformity to the image of Christ.

7. Persistent rebellion leads to exclusion and punishment. Proverbs 29:1 states, "He who is often rebuked, and hardens his neck, will suddenly be destroyed, and that without remedy." First Corinthians 5 discusses the exclusion of an unrepentant brother. This principle agrees with the treatment of a scoffer (see Essay 8) and is appropriate as a final resort.

Sound discipline principles implemented in the home and school are the basis for emotional well-being at every level of development. First, they provide the student with secure constancy in his environment. Second, they assure the student that he is the object of unconditional love as teachers primarily train and then correct as necessary in the student's best interests. Third, this strong nurturing atmosphere allows the student to develop a positive sense of his own identity, a sense of right relationships with others, and a sense of how God responds to His children.

You may want to institute your own personal study of the Word of God on the matter of discipline. Trace the references listed in the essay and write out your understanding of the verses and lessons you need to learn for effective classroom management. Let the Lord guide your thinking and then choose one area which seems to be a particularly weak and ineffective discipline procedure. Maybe it's the failure to confront, yelling too much, spanking too often, intervening in natural consequences. Determine with the Lord's help to gradually change in this area.

Personal Challenges

76 Model for the students how to handle crises, disappointments, frustrations and anger. You want to always be a good example in both word and conduct, especially when things are not going so well. Remember, James said, "Count it all joy . . . ."

77 Be yourself. Be genuine. Do not feel that you must be Mr. or Miss Perfect. Students are quick to catch anything synthetic or false in our attitudes. At the same time, don't adopt a "Do as I say, not as I do" approach. Simply be the vessel God can use to influence their lives.

78 Children need a teacher—not a playmate. Be friendly always, but remember, familiarity breeds contempt. You can interact well with students without becoming one of them.

79 Keep in mind that your students' lives are God's work. Be partners with Him and their parents, but do not take on responsibility for what you cannot accomplish. As a reminder, post these three verses where you can read them:

> *"For we are His workmanship, created in Christ Jesus for good works, which God prepared beforehand that we should walk in them." (Ephesians 2:10)*

> *"For it is God who works in you both to will and to do for His good pleasure." (Philippians 2:13)*

> *"Being confident of this very thing, that He who has begun a good work in you will complete it until the day of Jesus Christ." (Philippians 1:6)*

Let bygones be bygones. Do not hold grudges from day to day or week to week. Let students know that they have a fresh start. Be aware that if you anticipate or expect bad behavior, you will not be disappointed. Students can sense a critical attitude toward them and are likely to live up to your expectations.

Be consistent. Nothing is more confusing to a student than when a teacher is vacillating in mood and manner. This environment creates an immediate need for proving the boundaries and will result in confrontations.

Be fair. Students differ in their abilities and needs; consequently, they should not have to be treated exactly the same, only in accordance with their needs. However, a perception of "innies" and "outies" will create problems. Don't play favorites.

Consider how to obey the command: "Do not provoke your children, lest they be discouraged" (Colossians 3:21). What angers and discourages your students? Most will say: not knowing what to expect, inconsistent reactions from adults, unfair treatment among peers, never getting an opportunity to tell their side of the story, never being able to please, someone being angry without explaining why, not being recognized when they have tried hard and done a good job. How about your students? What would they say?

Some Important
Don'ts

Don't let students, or parents, misunderstand your physical closeness, pats and hugs. A teacher must be friendly but professional, and above reproach in relationships with others.

Don't begin to dislike a student because of his or her actions. You can discuss your displeasure and disappointment with a behavior while maintaining a confidence in God's ability to enable the student to do right. No child is beyond the redeeming power of Christ. Additionally, God would not have put him or her in your presence without expecting, and enabling, you to have a positive influence in his life.

Do not show anger. If you feel irritations building, firmly establish control over your own emotions. Demonstrate that control with relaxed, positive body language, including slow gestures and a steady, calm voice. Postpone any disciplinary response until you are in control of your emotions, thoughts and behavior.

87 Do not argue. You can't win. There is no argument over what is right or wrong, or who has authority. You can explain and discuss but the moment an argument begins, the discussion is over. You need only to state your request and indicate that the student has the opportunity to make a choice—comply, or challenge—then face the consequences.

88 Do not belittle or use sarcasm with students. Anger and criticism are never motivators of good discipline.

Sometimes, you need to ask the Lord to help you see students through His eyes—He never loses patience, reproaches, thinks evil. He sees each one as potentials—given salvation and sanctification.

89 Do not raise your voice or practice other behaviors that students perceive as threatening to their well-being. In response to such a threat, their brains downshift to an emotional response level. While you may be lecturing on the benefits of cooperation, they are totally incapable of processing logical thoughts. Resolve the emotional conflicts first, then return to a higher cognitive consideration of reasons why some behaviors are desired and others are not.

Don't get caught in the "criticism trap." This is the way it works: Harsh words (generally uncharacteristic of you) bring about a desired response. For example, you raised your voice to say, "Be quiet!" and the students stopped talking. Unconsciously, a message was sent to your brain which said, "This worked and is worth trying again." When a similar occasion arises, you raise your voice without even thinking. Only this time, your words must be a slight bit harsher and louder to get the same response. After several similar interactions, you have gotten into a habit—called a "criticism trap," which grows more frustrating for you and less effective with your students. Identify and break the habit quickly.

Do not over-react and thus escalate a minor incident into a major confrontation. Avoid confrontations in front of other students.

Do not threaten any action which you can't or won't carry out. At the same time, if there are natural or logical consequences for wrongdoing, students should have full explanations and reminders of them.

93 Do not bribe, make deals or compromise your standards to win popularity. Setting up a reward system where students can earn points toward a special event is different from telling the students in the midst of the problem that if they will be good, you will let them out five minutes early.

94 Do not put students in a position of tattling on others. If you enter a room of chaos caused by a few, you might ask the ones who were not involved to stand. Address them positively then discipline the remainder privately.

95 Do not give repeated warnings regarding misbehavior. One reminder about the rule can be fair. However, a repeat incident within a short time period is cause for action. You don't have to be harsh, just consistent, for your students to learn that you mean business.

Essay 6:

"Train up a child in the way he should go, and when he is old he will not depart from it." (Proverbs 22:6 NKJV)

Discipline and disciple come from the same root word, discipulus, meaning to learn (discere) and to teach (docere). Jesus called twelve men as His disciples and spent three years teaching and training them to carry forth the Gospel. He was the Master, or Rabboni, from whom they learned the words and works of God. John, Peter, James and the other nine were followers. But like many students today, they often misunderstood, had to be told a second and third time, argued with the teacher, argued with each other, failed to pay attention, over-reacted, went to sleep, had to be corrected—one even failed completely. Still they were disciples, learners of the Way, the Truth and the Life.

Today the word "discipline" seems to imply punishment and thus has a negative connotation. While punishment is an important part of discipline, it is helpful to refocus on the word's broader meaning—making disciples. Your role in teaching is the same as Jesus' ministry on earth—to take a rough bunch of fishermen mixed with a cultured but misdirected group of leaders and teach them to follow the Lord. Your job has much more to do with training students to walk in the right way than with reacting after a wrong way is chosen. Your ministry is to make disciples of the Way. You primarily must instruct in the right way continuously and effectively so that right actions are a result of right thinking. This is the intent of Deuteronomy 6:6–7:

> "And these words which I command you today shall be in your heart; you shall teach them diligently to your children, and shall talk of them when you sit in your house, when you walk by the way, when you lie down, and when you rise up."

The goal of good discipline (actually, instruction) is the same for your students as it was for Timothy—that his knowledge of the principles of the Word of God made him wise unto salvation and thoroughly equipped for all good works (2 Timothy 3:14–17).

The process of discipline can be diagrammed as presented on page 71.

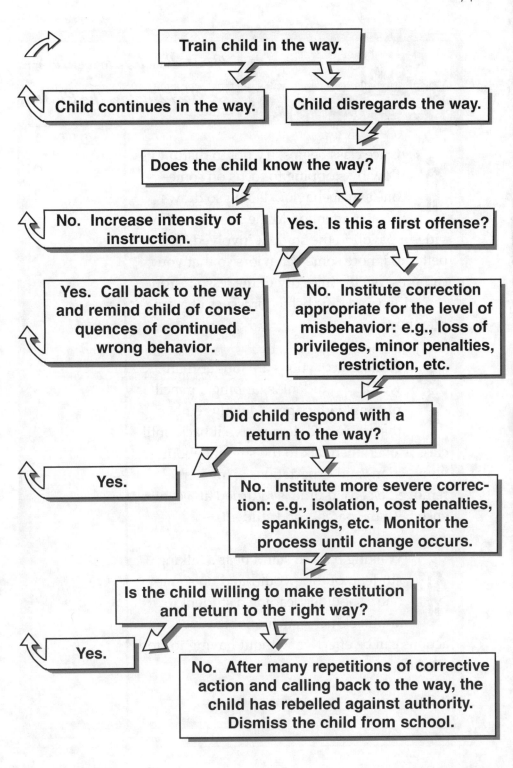

First Level Intervention—
Focusing on the Class

96 Once class begins, try not to disrupt its flow by stopping to focus on someone's misbehavior. Doing so draws greater attention to the offense and provides a payoff to the student involved. It's better to ignore some behaviors so that you can preserve the integrity of the lesson. You can address specific behavior issues at a separate time.

97 Sometimes, actions are louder than words. A student is tapping a pencil or playing with paper. Quietly remove the article and do not give it back until class is over; then talk to the student about your actions and expectations. Any item removed a second time is returned at a conference with the parents and student.

98 Walking back to stand near a talking student, putting your hand on someone's shoulder, leading a student to another chair—such unobtrusive actions can be effective without having to stop a lesson.

Try some silence. Stop dramatically in the middle of a word and wait for a student to comply. The group will sense the reason for your pause. Then go on without comment. If this alone is insufficient, check your watch and do a time count. The offending students then owe you time when others have proceeded to crafts, playground, music or lunch.

Try not speaking yourself until everyone is demonstrating desired behavior—not talking, in seats, etc. With older students, immediately open class at the bell with prayer or giving specific directions. If you are still talking with a co-teacher or looking for class materials, you have extended an invitation to continue talking.

Try lowering your voice—never raising it—so that students will have to make additional effort to hear you instead of talking or making noise. Avoid clearing your throat or blinking the lights. While these techniques may work initially, eventually students will be trained to assume that you are not really ready for class to begin until the telltale signal occurs.

If you get a negative response after giving directions, do not open the floor for negotiations. Turn, gain eye contact and clearly restate the directions followed by, "You can begin now." At a subsequent event, you can discuss the inappropriateness of such responses and your expectations that students will follow the directions provided.

Be aware that students often have a hard time distinguishing between times teachers are making suggestions and times they are giving directions. The messages are then mixed and confusion will result. Solve the problem by clearly stating which is which. The students won't have to ask questions for clarification or make guesses based on subtleties of voice or expression.

Not every question students ask is a challenge to authority, even when their voice tone has not conveyed the difference. Respond by simply asking the question, "Do you need additional information or are you challenging the instructions?" Your question indicates your openness, serves as a cue to change voice tone, and redirects a student's focus.

Try non-verbal techniques for some offending behaviors that occur: establishing strong eye contact, a slow shake of the head, a little grimace, slight move of the first finger, mouthing a warning, etc.

Essay 7: ## THE IMPERATIVE OF SUPERVISION

"The rod and reproof give wisdom, but a child left to himself brings shame to his mother." (Proverbs 29:15)

The most practical piece of advice for teachers in all of Scripture may be to remind us that students must be supervised. Any parent knows that when a toddler becomes too quiet, it's time to find out what is going on. Students—even teenagers—are going to get into trouble when left to themselves. Therefore, wisdom dictates the necessity to observe, interact and provide direction.

You need only to think of some experiences you or your friends have had to know how utterly naive it is of adults to think that it's okay to leave elementary students home alone after school, let junior higher go to the mall, or permit high school sweethearts to study in a bedroom.

Students function best with a high degree of accountability. Knowing that an adult is present provides security and defines the boundaries. For teachers, the issue is even more important since leaving students unsupervised can be considered negligence, a cause for a malpractice lawsuit if a student gets hurt.

Just determine that you will provide supervision for students entrusted to your care at all times. If a student gains permission to leave class but does not return on time, check on him. Your students will soon learn that you mean business when they must report to you. Preventing an incident because a student has been left to himself will ensure that he does not bring shame to his mother, or to you, his teacher.

106 Try praising a student who is demonstrating good behavior and compliment it. This serves as a reminder to another student without giving him attention for a negative act.

107 Try asking the student with offending behavior if you can help him. That gives you an opportunity to move closer, straighten his books and organize him for positive action.

108 If you have a student who finds it hard to maintain control, consider a private arrangement where you lay your pencil on her desk as a warning that her behavior is approaching unacceptability. When she regains control, walk by and pick up your pencil while giving a thumbs-up or a smile for reinforcement.

109 For a class that tends to be rowdy, try any one of a variety of reward systems. For example, with younger students you can place five removable stickers across the top of their desks. When an unacceptable behavior occurs, simply remove a sticker. Allow all students to earn back stickers they have lost, or to earn extra stickers, as they demonstrate desired behaviors. Whatever system you use, be sure it has positive aspects. For example, rather than putting

NOTES:

NOTES:

marks on the board for poor behavior, it is better to put up a number of marks or flags or stars, etc., for every student. You can then remove one if an offending behavior occurs. For your own sanity, make sure the system is easy to manage. With the stickers, for example, you can allow exchanges for free time or selections from a treasure chest after a certain number have been earned.

Keep some of your actions unpredictable. Don't call on students to read or answer questions in a routine. Skip around so that all students "stay on their toes." Remember to ask the question, then call on a student to answer after providing some "think time." You can help students who need more processing time by asking a question and indicating that you will return to them for an answer after you have asked a couple of other questions.

Be quick to change methodologies when you perceive students are tired of listening to you do all the talking. Try asking questions, implement a quick competition, have students stand and tell the main idea of the section to a neighbor, keep them standing while you proceed, set up a role-play to practice a skill or respond as the characters being studied. A change of pace can help you regain interest and participation.

Come alongside a student who is having trouble. Many students do better with a "guide by the side" rather than a "sage on the stage." Ask the Lord to help you develop this paraclete ministry of the Holy Spirit. Privately work out some routines of assistance such as not calling on the student to answer orally unless you've approached his desk as a signal, lecturing with your notes placed on his desk with permission for him to copy them, providing copies of your notes, spending time in extra-help sessions, etc.

If you are speaking or presenting book material, structure the listening tasks for your students. Indicate that when you finish, they should be able to name the three main reasons for Gideon's victory, the assignment of troops at Chancellorsville, the three miracles Jesus performed, etc.

With younger students, a special detective puppet can watch over students, occasionally whispering in your ear. At the end of the story, the puppet names the students (all when appropriate) to be recognized for good listening. As a reward they line up first or get an extra pat on the head.

Emphasize again and again the basic life principle that choices have consequences. Hold open discussions about wise versus foolish choices, mature versus immature choices, and choices that lead to giving life rather than death. These discussions can grow from daily experiences or characters from literature. Be sure students can articulate why a choice is one way or another. For example, a student is complaining or being critical. Why is their choice leading to destruction and death?

If unacceptable behavior is widespread in your class, concentrate on the ringleader. If you can win him, others will follow. This may mean special effort as you make contacts outside the class.

If a large number of students in the class "got it wrong" whether in learning or behavior, assume the fault to be your own, especially if there is no evil intent apparent on their part. For example, your class should know not to talk in the hall. However, several members foolishly get out of hand. Instead of punishing the class as a whole, explain that it is obvious that you have failed to help them know (or remember) what is required. Therefore, they need instruction and practice. Take time to review the expectations and practice desirable behavior. Next time, remind the class of your expectations before leaving the room.

Recognize and encourage small increments of improvement in behavior. Sitting still for five minutes is better than the two minutes last week. Move students progressively toward your expectations for them.

Develop a list of key Bible verses or phrases which are applicable to your expectations. Long, tedious lectures are ineffective; even worse, they build resentment. Just insert a verse at appropriate times and let the Spirit do His work. Some that are useful are:

Live in peace with each other. *1 Thessalonians 5:13*

Rejoice in the Lord always. *Philippians 4:4*

Do everything without complaining or arguing. *Philippians 2:14*

The servant of the Lord must not strike. *1 Timothy 5:22a*

Don't share in the sins of others. *1 Timothy 5:22b*

Be angry and sin not. *Ephesians 4:26*

Let him who stole, steal no more. *Ephesians 4:28*

Let no corrupt (rotten) communication proceed out of your mouth. *Ephesians 4:29*

Avoid the appearance of evil. *1 Thessalonians 5:22*

Provide things honest in the sight of all men. *Romans 12:17*

Even a child is known by his doings. *Proverbs 20:11*

To him who knows to do good, and does not do it, to him it is sin. *James 4:17*

I will set nothing wicked before my eyes. *Psalm 101:3*

Be kind to one another, tenderhearted, forgiving one another. *Ephesians 4:32*

Hate what is evil, cling to what is good. *Romans 12:9*

We do not want you to become lazy. *Hebrews 5:12a*

The Lord hates . . . a proud look and lying tongue. *Proverbs 6:17*

Essay 8:

UNDERSTANDING STUDENTS

"My son, if you receive my words, and treasure my commands within you, so that you incline your ear to wisdom, and apply your heart to understanding; yes, if you cry out for discernment, and lift up your voice for understanding, if you seek her as silver, and search for her as for hidden treasures; then you will understand the fear of the Lord, and find the knowledge of God."

(Proverbs 2:1–5 NKJV)

The Bible in the book of Proverbs clearly details our discipline programs for three types of children: the simple, the foolish and the scoffer (scorner). For ease of understanding, the information has been placed in an outline form to include the Scriptural bases, the problem, the results and the response to each type.

The Simple

Problem

1. He is void of understanding.
2. He is unlearned.
3. He knows nothing.

Results

1. He often falls into mischief.
2. He is easily led astray.
3. He unknowingly enters the wrong way.
4. He is gullible.
5. He participates in folly and playfulness.

Response

1. Teach him to understand wisdom.
2. Provide examples of others' punishments.

Scriptural Basis

Proverbs 1:4; 7:1–3; 8:5; 14:15, 19:25; 21:11; 22:3; 27:12.

The Foolish

Problem

1. He knows the truth but despises wisdom, instruction and knowledge.
2. He knows the truth but denies it.
3. He knows the truth but distorts it.
4. He knows the truth but displays pride and arrogance in a wrong heart attitude that mocks it.
5. He knows the truth but delights in mischief and stirring up strife.

Results

1. A pratting fool will fall.
2. He will cause sorrow and shame to those responsible for him.
3. He will die for lack of wisdom.
4. His companions will also be destroyed.

Response

1. Do not continue instruction, rather rehearse and remind him of present knowledge.
2. Administer the rod—some form of strong punishment.
3. Do not give him a place of honor by laughing or telling about his misdoings.

The Foolish (continued)

Response

4. Do not argue with him or carry on long discussions of rationale. His problem is not lack of knowledge, it's lack of desire.
5. Isolate him, as necessary, to reduce his influence on others and their influence on him. This provides time to think.

Scriptural Basis

Proverbs 1:7, 22, 32; 3:35; 7:22; 9:6, 13; 10:1, 8, 10, 14, 21, 23; 12:15–16, 19–20; 14:1, 7, 9, 16, 24; 15:2, 5–6, 14, 20; 16:22; 17:10, 16, 20–21, 24–25; 18:2, 6; 19:1, 13; 20:3; 22:5; 23:9; 24:7; 26:3–12; 27:22; 28:26; 29:11, 20.

The Scoffer (Scorner, Mocker)

Problem

1. He despises reproof and rebuke.
2. He has a proud, haughty, rebellious attitude.
3. He responds to correction with a contentious, angry spirit.
4. He displays a mocking, belittling ridicule of the truth.

Results

1. He is an abomination to others.
2. He is a shame to his parents.
3. His eventual judgment is prepared by God and will be delivered by a cruel messenger.

Response

1. Don't continue instruction or reproof after you have determined that he has passed from being foolish to being a fool.
2. Consider alternative placement that isolates him from the rest of the group. This can be in-school suspension or home based if his parents can provide close supervision.

The Scoffer (continued)

Response

3. Use the time to evaluate what should happen next. If the student chooses to repent and accept consequences, you can consider steps toward restoration.
4. If the student persists in unrepentance, dismiss him and trust that he will be disciplined by God.

Scriptural Basis

Proverbs 1:22; 3:24; 9:7–8; 13:1; 14:6; 15:12; 17:11; 19:25, 28–29; 21:11, 24; 22:10; 24:9; 29:8.

These three categories and their Scriptural instruction provide Christian educators a process for disciplining their students. The first and primary emphasis is on the instruction and training in the right way. The second course of action is correction and drawing back into the right way. The consistent application of these two principles will prevent most students from becoming scoffers.

However, there is a line of transition from the foolish child to the scoffer. Proverbs 17:10 says, "Rebuke is more effective for a wise man than a hundred blows on a fool." Notice the transition from foolish to a fool. Additionally, Proverbs 27:22 states, "Though you grind a fool in a mortar with a pestle, along with crushed grain, yet his foolishness will not depart from him." When this line is crossed, Proverbs 22:10 admonishes, "Cast out the scoffer, and contention will leave, yes, strife and reproach will cease."

With broken, sad hearts, teachers and administrators at times must release a student to the judgment of God. Admittedly, no Christian educator ever found this an easy experience; but real love, tough love, makes decisions on the basis of what can produce the greatest eternal benefit for a student.

*Second Level
Intervention—Focusing
on the Individual*

Proverbs says that foolishness is bound in the heart of a child. Therefore, it should not surprise or upset you that even in the best managed class, a student will make wrong choices. When these choices are repeated, and are not responsive to class intervention or gentle reminders, it is time to react on an individual basis.

Stay alert to the dynamics of your class as a whole and to its individual members. Try to catch problems before they occur. You see a student antsy or frustrated, move closer and provide direction or closer supervision. You see a couple of students on the verge of losing control, be ready to redirect their attention to an engaging activity. Many individual problems are preventable when a wise teacher is able to anticipate and intervene in potential problems.

Be discerning in determining when an undesirable behavior is really a problem. This usually involves the dynamics of intensity and time. In other words, how often does the misbehavior occur and how severe is it? Some questions to ask are: Is the behavior interfering with the student's learning? Is the behavior preventing others from learning? What would happen if I did nothing (will others imitate it)? Is the behavior interfering with the student's relationships with peers?

Being aware of the motivations for some misbehaviors helps in determining a correct response. For example, teachers report that the most frequent discipline problems they encounter are attention-seeking behaviors. When these occur and there is no payoff—no attention—the misbehaviors diminish. Therefore, it makes sense to conduct the class so that these behaviors are ignored, while at the same time, you build a positive relationship with the student and make sure he is getting attention for meeting your expectations.

Consider not intervening if an undesirable behavior will go away on its own, no one is being harmed or disrupted, and there is no ripple effect likely (other students imitating the same behavior).

Depend on natural consequences to correct some behaviors. If pieces of a game are lost or damaged, they are not available for further play. In other cases, depend on logical consequences. Two

preschoolers fussing over a toy results in the
toy being put away for a week. Items left on
the floor become the teacher's for two days.
Little explanation is needed for students to
understand and correct their actions.

When responding to a student who has
become emotionally upset, try some
emotional coaching techniques. Help
the student identify what she is feeling
and why. Talking about it diffuses strong
emotions. Identify and sympathize with the
feelings using statements like "I know it's
tough when you don't do as well as you had
hoped" or "You're right, nobody likes for others to call them names." When the student
senses that you have "come alongside" them,
shift the conversation to what problem is
faced now and what can be done about it.
Solicit the cooperation of the student in getting back on track.

With older students you can use peer
pressure to an advantage. If the wrong
was against the class, consider their
involvement in discussing why certain
behaviors are upsetting and interruptive.
They can suggest penalties. With high schoolers, peer mediation or courts can be effective.

In directing that an offending behavior
be stopped, avoid verbal attacks such
as "You are always . . . ." Instead use

NOTES:

an effective "I message." The four parts are:

- an objective description of the unacceptable actions. "When you make
noise with your pencil . . . ,"
- an expression of your feelings. "it
makes me feel annoyed . . . ."
- a description of the effect. "because it
breaks my concentration."
- a direct request to stop. "Please stop."

 Use a technique of redirection when
you observe that a student is reaching
or has reached the line of unacceptable
behavior. Be directive with a "Stop,
Focus, Go" command. "Stop tapping your
pencil, pick up your red pen and underline
the words I say. Ready? Begin."

 When a behavior is offensive, be firm
toward the actions but be friendly
toward the student. Don't hesitate to
make your expectations clear. "That
tone of voice must stop right now; but you
know what, I really like you and am convinced
that you are capable of using a polite voice
when requesting what you need. Try again."

 Be as brief as possible when asking a
student to stop an undesired behavior.
Stopping class to attend to the problem
gives the offending student power.

Intervene quickly and firmly, then move on. Save further correction for a more private time as long as the student is compliant at the moment. Be sure to follow up later so that you can clearly articulate your expectations, provide warning or implement punishment. Don't just "leave things hanging."

When being corrected, students often want to change topics and redirect your focus. Simply respond, "That's not the topic of conversation at this time. The issue is . . . ."

Some students want an unending discourse when discussing all their reasons for a misbehavior or their disagreement with your actions. While you want to receive and give as full an explanation as possible, at some point you must say, "I don't need to know if you agree. I need to know if you understand the problem."

For a student who continues a stream of "but . . . but . . . but," or openly resists your request, ask for clarification. "Help me understand, please. I have asked you to report to the office and you are refusing. Is that correct?" Usually the question refocuses the central issue and allows a pause, after which you can redirect the student. "Please report to the office. Thanks."

Some misbehaviors occur because students forget or foolishly choose to step out of the way you have defined for them. They need to be drawn back to the way and warned of consequences that result from a similar choice in the future. Eventually, if they "dance," they must "pay the piper." Impose the penalties you have available to you, trying to select the one that is likely to teach the best lesson in the least amount of time.

Usually a church or school has adopted a range of penalties that teachers may use. These generally include:

- losing a privilege such as computer time, snacks for a week, having a chair to sit in
- missing all or part of a desired activity— e.g., playground time
- time out—progressing from in the room, in the hall, in the supervisor's office, in a designated room
- staying after class
- earning demerits
- losing points toward a final grade
- detention, extra study hall or Saturday classes
- extra work such as writing assignments, special research, cleaning, raking leaves
- being placed on restriction, losing privileges to attend after-class events

NOTES:

- making restitution such as money to pay for damage to property, letters of apology, helping someone to make up lost time
- having others involved such as the principal, parents or pastor
- asking the parent or another adult to sit with the student in class
- removing the student from class for one-on-one supervision or alternative programming

Repeat offenses should result in increased penalties to the point that the price is one the student is unwilling to pay and thus serves to motivate the student to make right choices in order to avoid the consequences.

Respond quickly, consistently and decisively to issues related to character development. For example: unkindness, sullenness, whining, huffs, rolling eyes, purposeful disobedience, open rebellion. Make it clear that the student's words, attitude or actions are not acceptable and won't be tolerated. Follow through with consequences as soon as possible following a private conference.

Exercise any number of options to work with a student, or a small group of students, privately.

NOTES:

• coming to your desk
• stepping into the hall
• remaining behind when others have gone to the playground
• arranging to keep the student after school
• meeting in the supervisor's office
• asking a parent to join you

These are increasingly intense options for you to consider.

Essay 9:

TO SPANK OR NOT TO SPANK

"Foolishness is bound up in the heart of a child, but the rod of correction will drive it far from him." (Proverbs 22:15 NKJV)

There is a tremendous amount of misunderstanding on the topic of spanking in both public and Christian sectors. Whatever the prevailing attitudes among psychologists and social agencies, it would be very wrong for a Christian to disregard the counsel of God which clearly states, "He who spares his rod hates his son, but he who loves him disciplines him promptly" (Proverbs 13:24). However, this in no way condones child abuse since Christians are specifically forbidden to embitter or discourage their children.

Perhaps the clearest principles on this topic are Proverbs 22:8 and 22:15 where the "rod of correction" is contrasted with the "rod of anger." It is absolutely impermissible for an adult, just because he is larger, to lash out at a child in anger. This behavior only models that powerful, angry people can take out their vengeance on the most helpless among us. No wonder we have a crisis of violence, terrorism and crime in our country. This practice is not supported in Scripture, where we are as strongly restricted from anger as we are encouraged to correct children. In fact, we would have to agree that it is better never to strike a child than to strike one in anger.

The Biblical mandate is simply this: While the "rod of anger" will fail, the "rod of correction" will benefit a child. With that in mind, here are some guidelines:

1) Be knowledgeable of the laws of your state and the policies of your church or school. No matter how you feel personally, you do not have authority for spanking a child unless it has been specifically granted.

2) Only a parent, or a person acting in place of a parent, who has a long-term positive relationship with a child (caregiver, classroom teacher, principal, houseparent, etc.), should consider spanking a child. Non-parents should have specific permission from parents to administer a spanking.

3) Spanking should be reserved for serious offenses which have implication for character development and life-long habits.

4) The frequency of spanking should diminish as a child grows older. A stinging couple of swats on a preschooler's bottom can be most appropriate and can prevent major problems later. A spanking above elementary age should seldom, if ever, occur.

5) A child should never be struck angrily or hastily. The adult should be sure he is in control and that any punishment administered is done for the long-term benefit of the child, not to diffuse the anger or frustration of the adult.

6) The child should understand clearly what the offense was and why he or she is getting a spanking.

7) No one should be out of control. If a child (around age 4 and above) is fighting or crying hysterically, or otherwise out of control, wait it out. Place the child into isolation and determine that absolutely nothing else happens until the problem is resolved. That includes meals and other regular activities. As soon as the child is calm, pick up with an explanation and lead to his or her own confession of wrongdoing. Explain that you love him or her and care too much to allow behavior of that nature to continue.

8) Use a paddle or switch (rod) except for very young children (2 to 3 years) when a swat with an open hand can be effective. The number of swats and their intensity depend on the age of the child and whether this is a repeated wrongdoing. Typically, they range from one to three swats for a small child and three to five for an older child. Spank only the fatty part of the buttocks or upper thigh.

9) Tears are a refreshment for the soul and a sign of genuine sorrow. This is the response that you are looking for, and it should be rewarded. It is fine to sit and hold the child until the crying stops. Reassure the child of your love and your confidence that she is going to live up to your expectations in the future.

10) The student should be led to discuss and follow through with any apologies or restitution that is in order.

11) What's done is done. Do not repeatedly remind the child of the incident.

12) If a person other than the parents spanks a child, a detailed report of the incident should be made to the parents as soon as possible. A copy of the report should be kept in permanent records.

Spanking is a subject about which each person must be fully persuaded in his own mind. If needed, it must be used sparingly since there are few options to exercise after you have reached this one. If over-used, spanking loses its effectiveness. Therefore, it is best to begin early to impress on young students that this is an experience to be avoided at all costs. They are then more amenable to less intense forms of discipline.

As you discuss a persistent or intense problem privately with a student, follow the steps suggested:

1) Give a clear explanation of wrongdoing. Relate it to the damage done to the class or himself, not just a personal offense against you.

2) Try to get agreement on what the specific wrongdoing was. Ask the student to explain the problem in his own words.

3) Generally avoid questions like: "Why do you act like that?" He seldom knows! Most misbehaviors are born out of emotional needs, not rational thinking.

4) Assure the student that you believe he or she can meet your expectations for getting along in the class. Try to secure agreement on this point.

5) Just to make sure the student understands, review the expected behavior. Be as specific as possible. Again ask for a commitment to behave in a way that helps, not hurts, the class and himself.

6) Remind the student that the choice of any behavior is also a choice of the consequences it brings. Lead the student to an agreement that he chose the punishment when he chose the behavior.

7) Sometimes the timing is right—sometimes not—to explore the student's personal relationship with the Lord. Rely fully on the leadership of the Holy Spirit as you direct the student to repentance and acceptance of Christ as personal Savior. At the same time, do not use the offense to "beat the youngster over the head." It is the goodness of God that leads to repentance, and true repentance brings peaceable fruit of righteousness. You can't force this onto a student. It must be a work of grace in his life.

8) Assure the student of your interest and desire for him to be in your class. Indicate that you love the student and see great potential in life as he develops a heart for God and personal self-discipline.

9) Share consequences for continued problems if you feel it is necessary.

10) Implement the punishment associated with the wrongdoing.

NOTES:

Following one or two instances in which you have conferenced privately with a student of at least primary age, consider developing a contract for specific behavior. Write it out clearly with the expectations and consequences agreed to by both the student and teacher. A third party can witness it. Agree to a date for review and provide a copy to the student. Be sure to act on the basis of the contract.

 Part of a contract, or just an agreement with a student after a private talk, can be to establish an unacceptable behavior signal. This might be tapping your pencil on a desk or a quiet cough which to that student means a behavior is nearing unacceptability. Other students are unaware of this code. This is sometimes helpful in teaching a student how to monitor his or her own actions.

 If the student repeats an offense within a short period of time, or is persistently involved in other problems, continue the private consultations but increase the intensity of your interactions and the penalties associated with punishment.

 Isolation, time-outs and in-school suspensions are effective penalties. The amount of time should vary, depending on the age of the students.

Generally it should range from a ten-minute sit-out to suspensions of one to several days. During this time, the student loses all privileges and opportunities for social interaction. The same type of discussions, repentance, and restoration as in a spanking procedure should be implemented prior to the student returning to class.

Do not use penalties that are publicly humiliating to the child. Especially in a Christian school or church context where attendance is voluntary, you can do great harm to the cause of Christ in the life of a child. As a Christian, we never have the right to be offensive, even when working through the most difficult of circumstances.

Remember that the more time you invest on the front end of a problem, the more time you will save in the long run. Be willing to work with students individually until you have trained them in your expectations.

Commit to increased prayer for any student who seems to be unable or unwilling to follow the general expectations for others her age. Discipline problems seldom occur in isolation. The Holy Spirit can give you discernment regarding the root issues that are leading to persistent misbehaviors.

 Commit also to building a loving rela-tionship with the student. Be sure he doesn't anticipate every interaction with you to be punishment. Balance the times of negative interactions with times of encouragement and fun. Be his partner in a game during class. Arrange to go for a soda after class or to share dinner with his family. Go watch his baseball game. Make it important to him to want to please you.

 Do not talk to other people. It is dam-aging to the reputation of the student, an infringement on the parents, and a detriment to the body of Christ.

 Do not hesitate to contact parents. They like to be made aware of a prob-lem before it has had time to escalate. This is usually after you have had the first, or at the most, the second private con-ference. At this stage just alert them that the two of you are working on a problem related to talking without permission or forgetting homework, etc. Encourage them to encour-age the student in the progress he is making in solving the problem.

Take care in your approach to parents. When you are obviously upset, or busy dismissing students, and make a comment like, "Johnny was just impossible today," or "He is driving me crazy!"—you have just committed suicide on a relationship. Parents must perceive that there is no adversarial relationship between you and them. You both are on the same side. If you don't attack, they will generally not become defensive. Just say, "We are having some problems, and it would help if we could sit down and talk." Choose the time and place, and be prepared to give specific examples of the problem behaviors and what you have tried to do to correct them. Be open to suggestions from the parents and solicit their support as you assure them of your love and concern for their child.

Enlist parents as allies, especially in rewarding an improved or good report. However, it is unfair to expect parents to solve the discipline problems in your classroom. That is your job. Often parents will indicate that they want a daily report and a teacher shifts the burden of follow-up to the parents. Actually, what parents mean is, "We want to hear that he or she is doing better." A continuous negative report will disrupt your relationship with them and end with a lack of confidence in your ability as a teacher to positively manage the outcome for their child.

Some parents will want to be actively involved in administering penalties, especially when they understand the negative consequences a child will experience if the problems are not resolved. Be their partner in calmly reporting your concerns and the issues. Agree to a workable reporting system so that they will have needed information as they follow through at home.

Remind students who are resisting compliance that a parent conference is automatic with you when such situations occur. If you have a tape recorder handy, you may want to set it in front of the student and indicate that since you want to convey to parents exactly what was said, you would like permission to record your conversation.

Do your best to avoid escalating a potentially explosive situation. Some behaviors that produce unwanted results are:

- attempting to handle a matter while others are watching
- jumping to conclusions

NOTES:

- showing your own disgust
- letting your anger get out of control
- reminding students of past, forgotten offenses
- talking louder
- grabbing or jerking any part of a student's body
- nagging, moralizing
- accusing falsely
- disgracing or humiliating the student
- using subjective overstatements
- not allowing students to make a full explanation
- not allowing a student to "save face"
- being sarcastic, deriding or "talking down"
- criticizing or making negative comparisons to others
- involving unrelated people in the conflict
- making threats that you can't implement
- crying or otherwise losing control
- drawing a line and daring the student to cross it

Recognize that persistent misbehavior is often a sign of deeper need, usually related to a growing insecurity or the need for love. By fulfilling basic emotional needs (love, affirmation, belonging, self-esteem, purpose, positive contribution),

you may dismantle the need a student has to
disrupt the class. Meeting legitimate needs
will diminish a student's efforts to try to sat-
isfy those needs in unacceptable ways.

When problems persist, consider log-
ging behaviors and interactions. This
gives you a historical record and
becomes invaluable in assessing
whether there are triggers to misbehavior or
some pattern in their occurrence. For example, while intake of sugar is not a problem for
most students, some experience hypoglycemic
reactions including super resistant behavior
two hours following ingestion. A log that
records dates, times, behavior and reactions
can lead to diagnosis and effective treatment.

Essay 10: THE REWARDS OF DISCIPLINE

"No discipline seems pleasant at the time, but painful. Later on, however, it produces a harvest of righteousness and peace for those who have been trained by it." (Hebrews 12:11 NIV)

At some point our understanding of discipline as punishment is justified. We have a human nature bent to seek its own, to find pleasure in the world, and to ignore the needs of others. Even as God's children we can expect discipline, rebuke and punishment. In the midst of it we are told to respond correctly. The following principles are gleaned from Hebrews 12:5–11.

1) Don't make light of it. How easy it is to discount or laugh off the workings of God in our lives, especially when they come through human instruments. God has one goal for us—to be conformed to the character of His Son. He will do whatever it takes, including discipline whenever needed. We should not take His claims lightly.

2) Don't lose heart. Facing the consequences of our wrongdoing, including the disappointment of those who love use, can cause us to lose hope of ever successfully living by God's standard. Be encouraged! It is Christ in you, the hope of glory, and His energy

which so powerfully works (Colossians 1:27 and 29). We can do all things through Him who gives us strength (Philippians 4:13).

3) Endure hardship. Discipline is not pleasant, but painful. Escape and avoidance are natural human reactions. However, we are encouraged not to give up. In the end discipline has a perfecting purpose. If we truncate the process too quickly, the lesson usually has to be relearned at a later time.

4) Submit to the process. The challenge is to be participants in what God wants to accomplish. We need to react on the basis of two questions: What do I need to learn, and how should I respond? The sooner we respond as God wants, the sooner we are restored to righteousness and joy.

These principles have great importance as we respond to God and as we teach students to positively respond to human discipline.

The passage in Hebrews 12:5–11 also provides some encouragement to the administrators of human discipline.

1) Discipline is a result of love—of wanting the best for the child involved. If we didn't care, we could ignore a wrongdoing, assuming it is someone else's problem. It is our concern that motivates

us to correct inappropriate attitudes and actions, even when it's not convenient or easy. Our model is God who disciplines us for our good.

2) We discipline as we think best. That's all we can do. Sometimes we will make mistakes, have to apologize and try to make restitution. We can improve as we learn and experience better methods. Ignorance and ineptitude can't be an excuse when we are working with lives that are precious to God.

3) Discipline produces a harvest of righteousness and peace. What a promise! The end result of discipline will be restoration to right behavior. A peaceable spirit then encompasses the child. This is when we know our efforts have been effective.

God's Word clearly defines punishment as an aspect of discipline. Unwanted but often needful, it can be effective in bringing a student back into a peaceable habitation.

"All your children shall be taught by the Lord, and great shall be the peace of your children." (Isaiah 54:13 NKJV)

Seeking Help

If problems persist, consult with your supervisor at the point that you feel ineffective in correcting the student. This is usually when you have had to warn a student in class or have had several private talks, and things are just not working. The supervisor can help you decide alternative approaches, determine when parents should be involved, and seek help from other sources.

If a student persists in misbehavior and is unresponsive to discipline, more serious steps should be taken to diagnose possible emotional conflicts, attention deficit disorders, learning problems or other underlying causes. Here are some suggestions:

1) Have a conference with your supervisor, the parents and other specialists you have access to in order to review the problems encountered.

2) Refer the parents and student to a professional child psychologist in whom you have confidence.

3) The student can receive professional evaluations and recommendations for treatment.

4) The student and his family can be provided professional counseling.

5) If your class is not the most appropriate educational environment for the student, a recommendation can be made for transfer into a setting which offers a better class placement and a more comprehensive array of services.

While Christian teachers are generally long on love and patience, a student who continues to disrupt the educational climate of a classroom must at some point be dismissed. The quality of the program and the good for the majority of students may result in the exclusion of one or two students who cannot be served in your setting. Often this drastic action is the catalyst for the student to receive needed services.

*Final
Encouragements*

Keep your words at a minimum and make them count. Solomon's advice was, "A man of knowledge uses words with restraint, and a man of understanding is even tempered" (Proverbs 17:27) and "The more the words, the less the meaning, and how does that profit anyone?" (Ecclesiastes 6:11 NIV).

Do not be afraid to show a sense of humor. Some situations are very funny and you cannot avoid them. Laugh with your students. Obviously, there is a difference in laughing at a situation and laughing at a person— which is never allowed. Laughing at yourself when you "mess up" is a good role model for what students should do when they "mess up."

Be big enough to admit mistakes, make apologies both publicly and privately, and be a good example of how to start over.

Make contacts outside of class: a phone call, post card, or a short letter are demonstrations of your love for your students. Sometimes you might provide an addressed, stamped envelope for a student to write you a note. Promise to answer any letters you receive. Encourage note writing and written encouragement within your class.

Send home positive reports, not just negative ones. Notes, report forms, awards, smiley faces stamped all the way to the elbow—these are great! Consider asking the principal to write a letter to the parents of an older student who has been making great progress.

Researchers say that, in general, teachers give three times as many negative communications as positive. Don't get bogged down in the negative. When you sense your interactions with students leaning more and more to the negative, take stock! At the end of each day you should feel that you have had at least as many positive as negative interactions with every student.

As a final note, discipline is a marvelously positive process. The truly unresolvable problems are small in

NOTES:

number. Therefore, keep your perspective. Actually, "this too shall pass" are comforting Biblical words.

Finally, be patient! God is not finished with your students (or you) just yet. It takes time to work out problems, and it takes time to build a relationship in which you can have a positive influence in the lives of your students.

Essay 11:

THE PASSION TO TEACH

"What we have heard and known, what our fathers have told us, we will not hide them from their children; we will tell the next generation the praiseworthy deeds of the Lord, his power, and the wonders he has done. He decreed statutes for Jacob and established the law in Israel, which he commanded our forefathers to teach their children, so the next generation would know them, even the children yet to be born, and they in turn would tell their children. Then they would put their trust in God and would not forget his deeds but would keep his commands."
(Psalm 78:3–7 NIV)

Why are you a teacher? For the short hours? lucrative pay? high prestige? gratefulness of students? "Ha!," you say. The truth is that there is only one reason for you to be a teacher. That is the call of God. In fact, James warns that most people should not seek to be teachers, because stricter judgment awaits those who teach (3:1).

Teaching is a high calling to invest your life in things of eternal value—the Word of God and the souls of people. If not for a dedication to ministry, it would be easy to give up when things get tough. The long hours of preparation, the hard work, the constant challenge of discipline, the heart-wrenching concern for the few students who seem unreach-able—nothing would make these worthwhile except for the love of Christ

shed abroad in your heart and a passionate desire to teach this generation the wonderful words and works of our Lord.

Jesus said, "A student is not above his teacher, but everyone who
is fully trained will be like his teacher" (Luke 6:40). Teaching is a process
of imprinting life to life. The picture is one of molding clay where you
might leave a thumbprint as you sculpt a worthless lump into an object of
usefulness. Jesus' words contain both promises, as well as some warnings.

1) Teaching is productive; it accomplishes a life-changing work.
Probably no other career is as rewarding as teaching. It is sheer pleasure to watch students learn. At the same time, like the parable of
the sower, the productivity of the seeds can vary in its amount of
fruit. Our challenge is to trust God for the increase.

2) The end result of your teaching may not be apparent immediately.
Students are in the process of becoming. We must be satisfied to
work on the foundation according to His plan, knowing that God has
an ultimate plan which He will accomplish in their lives.

3) Students become like their teachers. How do you feel about having
clones of yourself? Most of the truly important lessons for life are
caught, not taught. Worldview, values, how to handle frustration and
failure, starting over, being persistent, caring for others—these and

thousands of other character traits are gleaned from the lives of significant adults who influence students. What a challenge to us to be the models that will establish students in the ways of God.

Considering our responsibilities as teachers could be discouraging if it were not for the fact that we are co-laborers together with God. In Luke 6:38 we have a wonderful promise: "Give, and it will be given to you. A good measure, pressed down, shaken together and running over, will be poured into your lap. For with the measure you use, it will be measured to you" (NIV).

While teaching has its earthly rewards, the person returning the blessing is God Himself. Since He will be a debtor to no one, you can trust the fact that the return on your investment in the lives of students will be beyond measure. Trust Him, be conscientious in your daily responsibilities, reflect His nature, persevere—you will be rewarded both in time present and in eternity.